Blogging
Million Dollar Blogger

Zachary Eddlestein

Introduction

What this book is going to show you is exactly what you need to do to get your blog monetized in exactly the same way that million dollar bloggers monetize their blogs.

It doesn't matter if you're coming in blank and have no idea about how to start a blog at all, or if you've been blogging for years but just are not sure how you should be monetizing things. This book will take care of your needs in either case.

Could you start a million dollar blog with what you learn in this book? You most definitely can, as this book shows you how to do exactly what the big million dollar bloggers are doing. That said, I don't want to mislead you into thinking that you should quit your job today because you'll suddenly have a million dollar blog. That's not how this works, it takes time to develop your blog into a million dollar blog. Also, how successful you are largely depends on the work you put in, the demand of the market, how much competition is coming into your niche, and a trillion other little factors that are difficult to measure.

Thus, this book does not guarantee that you will earn a million dollars with your blog. Though, if you do what this book says, you'll be in the best possible position with your blog to be able to get it to that point, as you'll understand exactly how the million dollar bloggers do it, and exactly how you'll need to do it.

Even if you implement everything in this book and don't earn a million off the bat, you should still be in a very good position to earn something. As there are many who earn hundreds, thousands, and even hundreds of thousands with their blogs who are not even using the strategies taught in this book. Thus, you'll be a bit more advanced than them by the time you get through this book, so you're highly likely to achieve some level of success if not an actual million dollar blog, as long as you follow the instructions given in this book and don't deviate from them. And that's kind of all there is to it.

However, if you only partially implement the things taught in this book and you don't see results, then you can only blame yourself. Therefore, I would suggest that you do not take what you learn here and just kind of implement it. Look, you have to be all in on this! If you're not all in, then the odds are highly likely that you will fail! It's as simple as that!

However, if you are all in! Well then, the blogosphere is your oyster! There's nothing quite like having a million dollar blog paying you a passive income each and every month, so getting your blog to the million dollar mark is definitely a goal worth striving for, so be prepared to be dazzled, because I'm going to show you exactly what you need to do! Are you excited? I didn't hear you say Yes! Was that a Yes? Well, absolutely splendid then, so am I, so let's get this show on the road!

Table of Contents

About The Author

My name is Zachary Eddlestein, and I blog for a living. It wasn't always like that though.

I used to work a job, and I'm not going to say that my story was a rags to riches story, because it very much wasn't. And I don't really want to bore you too much with it, so to make a long story short, I was a sales executive in a Fortune 500 company, and I thoroughly loved my job. I was one of the best at what I did. I made a lot of money, lived an above average lifestyle, and was completely happy.

Though what happened to me is that I was suddenly struck with an extremely rare kind of disability, one that no longer allowed me to work at an office. I felt too proud to go on disability, and didn't want to become an unemployed disabled person dependent on the system, so I knew that I had to figure out something else.

I knew that I wanted to work online, but I wasn't sure exactly what kind of online work would be best for me. After months of research at home on my computer, and considering all sorts of possible ways I could make money online. I decided that the ideal option for myself would be that of blogging.

Why blogging? Well, I've always had a knack for writing, and I simply admired the kind of lifestyle that many of the big name bloggers were living. They lived life on their terms, they worked when they wanted, blogged when they wanted, and the money seemed to keep on rolling in. They were living the dream in my eyes.

I thought long and hard about why everyone wasn't doing it? I mean, it seemed easy enough for anyone to just write their own career by learning to blog, so why wouldn't everyone just start a blog and make the big bucks? And what I came up with is that first of all, not everyone wants to write blog posts for a living! And second of all, not everyone is willing to keep at it! Most people easily get bored and give up at the slightest sign of difficulty in whatever they do, and then just move on to the next thing. However, that wasn't going to be me, I vowed, I would become the most determined blogger ever! I would make it at blogging or die trying! And that is exactly what I did, I made it!

I hope that each and every one of my students also has the will, desire, strength, and fortitude to make it as well! It's definitely not an easy path, but the rewards are well worth the effort!

Chapter 1: Million Dollar Bloggers

Bloggers are people who write for a living, but they don't write books or anything like that. Rather they write blog posts, which is more akin to writing news articles than anything else. The only real difference between a blog post and a news article is that news articles are written for the general population at large, whereas blog posts are written for those who are specifically into some kind of particular niche.

There are many levels of bloggers. There are plenty who start blogs but never follow through. There are many successful low level bloggers who earn about as much as a part-time job. There are many mid-level bloggers who earn about as much as a full-time job. Then there are your elite bloggers, those who earn upwards of six figures, and some of which have crossed the million dollar threshold qualifying them as a million dollar blogger!

Million dollar bloggers are a bit different than the rest in the way they set things up, and in the strategies they implement. And that's what this book aspires to teach you, it will teach you everything you need to do in order to set up and run a blog in very much the same way as a million dollar blogger does it. Now, whether you actually do it or not is another matter.

The strategies which this book teaches are not anything I've come up with, rather they are the strategies of real world million dollar bloggers. All I'm doing is simply breaking it all down into bite-sized chunks for you to easily absorb. How successful you are with these strategies largely depends on yourself, and the time and energy that you put into implementing them.

In any event, as long as you read this book through cover to cover, you'll know exactly what the million dollar bloggers are doing, and you'll know exactly how to do what they do. Thus, you'll have the entire plan to basically replicate what a million dollar blogger does. Though it's entirely up to you what you do with it!

How bad do you want it? That's what it comes down to. Sure you can take some of the strategies in this book and put together a very well-to-do blog, but you really need to tackle the yeti head-on, grabbing him by the horns and headbutting him into submission if you're shooting for a million dollar blog.

I should also say that anyone that has a million dollar blog works their tail off to keep it going, as it's not an easy thing to maintain by any means. And with that, let's dive right into it!

Chapter 2: Niche

A million dollar blogger should not only write to a specific audience, but also needs to be the audience. Therefore, when you are considering what niche you should create a blog on, the best niche is going to be the one that you would be interested in reading a blog on yourself.

Thus, before you even think of choosing a niche, let's imagine that you have an hour of free time right now, and you have no choice but to read a blog for that hour. What kind of blog would you read? A blog about gadgets? A blog about diets? A blog about something spiritual?

Well, the kind of blog that you chose to read is exactly the kind of blog you need to create, because that's exactly the kind of blog who's audience you most understand the psychology of. After all, you are the audience!

If you're still not sure about it, then get on your computer right now and start looking for blogs you might be interested in. Come on now, it's easy, just go to Google or Bing and type in whatever-you're-interested-in followed by the word "blog." What comes up there in the results are the blogs of your competitors.

Go ahead, put this book down right now and start reading their blogs, and then come back when you're done.

If there is nothing you are interested in, and if you don't see yourself as being able to think like any audience, then you need to find yourself some interests. Sure you can follow the strategies in this book and create a blog in a niche you have no interest in, but I'll warn you now that it's a very clear path to failure, because you'll be highly likely to get bored with it and give up. Thus, before moving on, you should close this book and go find at least one thing that interests you, and then come back when you have one.

Have you got a niche yet? Do you know what you would like to blog about? If you're answers to these questions are all a definitive YES, then we're ready to move on!

Chapter 3: Product

Once you have your niche and you know what you want to blog about, the next thing you should be thinking about is your product.

A lot of people get it all wrong and start writing their blog and have no product whatsoever, and then they wonder about why they're not making any money. Well, it's quite obvious why you aren't making any money, isn't it? It's because you have no product!

Seriously though, before you even think about writing a single blog post, you need to think about what your product is.

The blog itself is not a product, your blog posts are free for people to read, so you can't make money with your blog alone, so you most definitely need a product.

While it's possible to sell almost any kind of product, we're going to be focusing on the 2 types of products that most million dollar bloggers promote, and they are:

Digital Information Products

A digital information product is anything digital that you can sell which contains information. It could be an ebook, audio book, video course, or anything else.

The great thing about digital information products is that unlike physical products you won't run out of stock, and you also don't have to worry about shipping charges or defective items or anything like that. This is the beauty of selling information.

The next question you might be wondering is where you're going to get an info product to sell? Well, it's quite simple, you make it!

Don't make the mistake of selling an info product made by someone else, as it will cause your followers to think less of your blog and more about that other person. You have to be the one to make your own info product. However, don't worry, it's not hard.

As a first product, I'd recommend to create an ebook. To create that, all you have to do is write up something in your word processor and export it as a PDF file, and you have a product.

The simplest products tend to be short instructional guides that explain how to do something related to your niche. It should take you only a few hours to create one, perhaps 2 days at the most. Such a short guide would make a fabulous first product!

When you create your first product, you want to make sure it's directly related to your niche, it provides a high degree of value, and it's high quality with no grammatical errors.

It may take some thinking time to decide what your first

product is going to be, so it would be good to start thinking about it.

Affiliate Products

An affiliate product is a product that someone else or a company made.

The way it works with an affiliate product is that you first of all have to find affiliate programs. You can find these by typing in keywords related to your niche into a search engine followed by the words "affiliate" or "affiliate program."

Once you find an affiliate program related to your niche, you need to find the registration button, which will be somewhere on the page explaining about the affiliate program, and register for it.

It's best if you register with about 3 to 6 affiliate programs to start with, and then register with more later. It would also be good if you make a list of affiliate programs that you find related to your niche.

The way an affiliate program works is that once you register, you'll be given login access to an affiliate dashboard. Once inside the affiliate dashboard you should have access to affiliate links and banners.

You want to copy those links and banners and later put them on your blog. And when someone goes to your blog and clicks on one of your affiliate links or banners and makes a purchase, you will be paid a percentage of the purchase price.

It's really quite a beautiful system that allows you to have a product without actually having a product. However, since million dollar bloggers have both their own products and affiliate products, so should you!

One very important note on affiliate links and banners:

The FTC, also known as The Federal Trade Commission, requires that we disclose our affiliate links.

I can recommend no better source to find out about how to do this properly than straight from the horse's mouth, the FTC themselves. I have a link for you to their policies regarding disclosing affiliate links at:

BloggerBlogger.com

Also, once you understand what you're doing as far as disclosing your affiliate links, I'd recommend checking your competitor's blogs and any other blog you stumble upon to see who is disclosing properly and who is not.

Lead Magnet

A lead magnet is very much like an info product that we would sell, and is usually a small ebook or report, but it could be anything. However, unlike an info product, our lead magnet is something which we will give away for free.

It may seem counter-intuitive to create an info product for the purpose of giving it away. However, we're not in the business of giving freebees, so rather than think of your lead magnet as a product, you should instead think of it as bait.

Thus, your lead magnet must be something with high value that anyone in our niche would really want to have. Therefore, it would be good to start thinking about what kind of lead magnet we could create.

We're not going to be giving it away entirely for free though, rather we're going to be exchanging it for email addresses.

If you've encountered one of those online free gifts that all you have to do is put your email into some form to claim, well then that's exactly what a lead magnet is.

Chapter 4: Your Competitors

The next thing we need to consider is what our competitors are doing and how they are monetizing their blogs.

We learned how to find our competitors in Chapter 2, so now we need to look at their blogs and analyze them. We need to analyze them from the perspective of "how are they making money?" Therefore, we want to find what products they are selling, if any. And we also want to look for where they're placing their affiliate links or affiliate banners, if any.

We want to check the affiliate programs they are using a note them down, and compare them with the affiliate programs we already know about.

We also want to examine how often each of our competitors is posting, as well as what kind of content they're writing blog posts about.

Based on what our competitors are doing, we can gauge what we ultimately need to do. Our goal is to become the number one authority blog in our niche, so anything our competitors are doing, we have to do it better.

We want to become the biggest fans of our competitors. We want to subscribe to their mailing lists in order to analyze their lead magnets, and also to read the emails they send us. Also, we want to bookmark their blogs in our browser, so we can check them every day for new posts. We should all the while be taking lots of notes about their activities. As they say, keep your friends close and your enemies closer. We want to be keeping our competitors very close.

If we wanted to get sneaky, and ask them questions about something we didn't understand, we could comment on their blog with a question using a name and email that wouldn't identify us.

We should never give away our true intentions! That we are in the midst of plotting to create a blog in this niche that will outdo theirs.

We want to ultimately launch a blog that is going to be way better than their blog, so we need to note everything that they do that we like.

We also want to check where our competitors are posting on social media, and if they have a Youtube channel or Facebook Group, or Facebook Page. We should be Googling their name trying to find any juicy bits of data we can on them.

Our analysis of our competitors could take a day or it could take weeks. This really depends on the size of our niche and on how many competitors we have. It's best if we are thorough in our research leaving no stone unturned, because ultimately we're going to use all of this data to out-smart them!

Chapter 5: Preparing

Now that we have data on our competitors, it's time we begin the preparatory phase of our plans.

Build The Product

If we haven't already done so, the time has come to build our info product. Likely this will be an ebook, but if we wanted to we could build something more complex like a video course.

Build The Lead Magnet

This should take a lot less work than building our product. Ultimately though, our lead magnet is something that should solve a problem for those into our niche, or at the very least teach them how to do something.

Once we have one info product and one lead magnet created, we're ready to move on to the next part of our plan.

Chapter 6: Tools

We need to next prepare our tools, and there are 3 we definitely need.

I will put my picks for these 3 tools at:

BloggerBlogger.com

Host

A host is a company that rents us the server space that serves our blog to the public. It's not free, but fairly inexpensive.

Premium Theme

Think of a premium theme as basically being a piece of software that allows us to design the look of our blog.

Autoresponder

An autoresponder is the service we need to build our email list and set up our lead capture form, the form we use to acquire emails. We give our lead magnet out to each person who gives us their email.

Chapter 7: Setup

We want to set up our hosting first. We should pick a domain name, and purchase hosting.

SSL

We then need to deploy an SSL certificate.

SSL stands for Secure Sockets Layer. In a nutshell it's basically a certificate that ensures that data passed between your blog and other places is secure.

It's a little thing, but worth mentioning, because most people overlook this point. It's another one of those things you need to take care of. In most cases however your host will set this up for you if you ask, and that's all you have to do with it. And if they won't set it up for you they most definitely will walk you through the process.

Just tell them, "Hey, I would like to make sure my SSL is set up." And they should oblige.

WordPress

We then need to install WordPress.

If you didn't already figure out how to install WordPress on your website, then bug your hosts support to help you figure out how to get it installed. They should be used to helping people set this up, because I'm pretty sure they get asked about this one daily.

Email

Another thing you want to set up is email. Again, your host's support should help walk you through this process, it's what you're paying them for. They should also help you to work things so that you can check your email from your mobile device. It's a breeze to setup if you just bug support about it.

Premium Theme

Then we need to purchase and install our Premium theme.

Autoresponder

Finally, we want to purchase a plan with our autoresponder and set up a form on our blog, so that when someone signs up they get a first email with our lead magnet.

Once we've completed this setup, we're golden!

Again, in case you missed it, you can find my picks for Hosting, Premium Theme and Autoresponder at:

BloggerBlogger.com

Chapter: 8 SEO

In case you didn't know, SEO stands for Search Engine Optimization, and that basically means making our blog easy to find on search engines. For example if we wrote a blog on horses, then when someone types "horses" into a search engine we want to come up on the first page.

What affects which page we come up on. Well, a few factors affect it, and they are:

Click Percentage

The click percentage is for example, when someone types "horses" in the search bar of a search engine and sees your blog, what percentage click on it versus what percentage don't.

Overall Blog Traffic

Overall blog traffic is how much traffic your blog is getting in general via searching for your listing on search engines as well as via people clicking links to it from elsewhere such as other websites, social media, and emails.

Interactivity

Interactivity is how many people who go to your blog actually click around inside your blog. The more people who click around inside your blog the better your blog will rank in the search engines.

Keywords

The more of certain keywords exist in your blog posts, the higher they'll rank in search engines.

Fresh Content

The more updated content your blog has, the better it will rank in search engines. That's why it's important to keep making new blog posts.

If you can get a handle on all the specific points I mentioned above, you'll do just fine with SEO.

Chapter 9: Getting Traffic

There are 3 primary ways that you're going to be getting traffic to your blog.

Writing Fresh Blog Posts

The first way you'll be getting traffic is by writing fresh blog posts. You need to come up with good content and come up with it regularly, and you need to write like the wind!

In the beginning you'll be making a lot of blog posts and feeling like no one is reading them or that nothing is happening. That's fine, just continue the process. Just keep writing blog posts, because over time you'll start to get traffic via search engines. The search engines love fresh blog posts, and with every blog post you write there is a chance to get traffic, as long as the search engines see that your blog is consistently posting fresh content, they'll start to notice you.

Now, it's important to note which blog posts of yours seem to be getting the most comments, because if certain blog posts are getting a lot of comments, and others are not, then it means you've hit a vein that many people are searching for. So what you want to do is to write more blog posts in the same area as the ones bringing you the traffic.

I think using comments to determine which blog posts are

getting the most traffic is fine at first, but eventually you want to make sure to register your blog with Google Analytics which will give you the real data on how much traffic each blog post is getting. If you're not sure where to find Google Analytics, just go to:

Analytics.Google.com

Social Media

Social media is a great way to get traffic to your blog. Now, with social media there are 2 ways to do things, you can do one or the other or both, it's totally up to you.

The first way is to use your own social media profile, and what you basically want to do is mention that you've just published a new blog post and place a link to it. You can do this by making a Facebook Post on your own profile, or on a Facebook Page, or in a Tweet, or in an Instagram post, or in a Youtube video, or on whatever social media platforms you use. It's totally up to you. Of course the more social media platforms you are a member of the better. You want to post a link to all of your platforms for each new blog post that you publish everytime you publish a blog post.

The second way to do it is if you wanted to conceal your identity. In that case you would simply create new social media profiles for either the name of your blog or for your pen name. And basically do the same thing, which is posting a link for each new blog post that you make.

By doing this you'll get some visitors to your blog, and by doing this with each new blog post that you put out, over time your social media profiles may turn into a neat little source of blog traffic for you.

Likewise, you'll also want to do the reverse, and put links to your social media profiles on each new blog post. This way anyone who is into your blog who wants to be notified every time you post a new post can easily just follow your Twitter, or your Facebook Page, or your Instagram, or subscribe to your Youtube channel, or follow or subscribe to any of your other social media platforms.

It's really up to you which social media platforms you decide to go with, but if you're really keen on growing your blog, then I would say just go ahead and join them all! After all, it's never going to hurt you, it can only help!

Forums

Forums are a great way to gain more followers. In order to find forums in your niche, you simply type in the name of your niche in any search engine followed by the word "forum." You should then see a number of results to various forums in your niche. If you don't see a number of results to various forums in your niche, then there are other places you can check such as Facebook groups or Reddit, communities which are basically like forums.

You want to join as many forums in your niche as you possibly can. Whether you join under your real name or under a pen name is entirely up to you.

Once you're a member of a bunch of forums, you want to choose up to 5 of the biggest ones, and be sure to drop in on them every day to see what people are posting, and to make your own posts.

What you basically want to do is become part of the scene of these forums. You want to be reading others posts and answering their questions, as well as writing your own posts. The goal you are going for is to be seen as an authority figure on the niche in each of the forums that you check daily.

Don't share links to your blog posts right away, instead just focus on becoming part of the scene. Eventually, it could take a few months, after you've built up a certain level of respect and authority, you want to then start sharing links to your recent blog posts.

Don't just blatantly share your blog posts for no reason though, and be sure to check the rules of each respective forum to understand how links should be shared.

One strategy for sharing a link to one of your blog posts is if someone asks a question in the forum, you respond saying that you've actually just recently written a blog post on that very topic and post a link to your blog post. What they won't realize is that after you read their question, you then went to work creating a blog post on the topic answering their question so that you would have an excuse to put a link in the forum. However, don't let them think that, just make it seem like a coincidence that you just wrote a blog post on that very topic.

Don't go overboard with putting links to your blog posts in the forums your in. You only need a few very well placed strategic links to gain a lot of traffic going to your blog from forums. Most importantly you want to be a part of the scene, and not make it look like you are only there in order to get traffic to go to your blog.

Also, with some forums, you may be allowed to put a link to your blog in your signature or on your profile page. And if that's the case, then this is great, because just by posting a lot in the forum, people who like what you have to say will click on your link in your signature or click to see your profile and find out about your blog.

If your blog looks like something amazing, they'll be impressed, and they'll have even more respect for your comments on the forum.

The Goal

With both social media and forums, you basically want to use them in the early stages of your blog to help gain an initial boost of traffic, so that the search engines rank your blog higher.

Once search engines rank your blog well enough that your getting most of your new followers off of search engine traffic, you want to slow things down on social media and forums, and put the majority of your focus on just writing great blog posts.

The goal is to just be able to write great blog posts and have that be enough to bring you all the traffic you need without having to rely on social media and forums. Though of course you should still be doing social media and forums!

Chapter 10: Search Engine Registration and Tracking Traffic

You want to first of all register your site with Google Search Console, which can be found at:

Google.com/Webmasters

It might be a bit of a learning curve to figure that out, but between Google's tutorials and pestering your hosting company repeatedly, you should be able to figure it out. It's simply one of the barriers of entry we have to go through to be bloggers.

A lot of people give up at this point, but don't give up, we all had to go through this, and you'll never have to do it again, so not to worry!

If you figure this one out, you'll be one of the 1% who didn't quit, so pat yourself on the back!

Ready for some more pain? Good! So if you haven't already, you next of all want to register with Google Analytics, which can be found at:

Analytics.Google.com

And you need to figure out how to install the Google Analytics plugin on your WordPress site, which is a breeze. Basically, you go to your WordPress dashboard, click on "Plugins" in the left sidebar and then "Add New" below it, and then type in the search bar "Google Analytics" and find the one made by Google, and then click "Install," and then click "activate" and you are done! See, piece of cake!

Then figuring out what to do with it is a whole other can of worms. Though it's all in Google's tutorials. No point for me to show you how, as no one is better to show you how to use Google's technology than Google themselves. So check their help in the plugin or on the Google Analytics website for that info. Again, this is another one of the barriers of entry you have to go through. Though it's not as tough as you think.

With Google Analytics you'll be able to track where all of your traffic is coming from. Tracking traffic is an art within itself, and worth taking the time to familiarize yourself with.

Why even bother with tracking traffic? Well, that's a good point, but look at it this way: Let's say you write 30 blog posts and most of your blog traffic is coming from one of those posts, well you'd want to know that, because if you knew that, you could be writing more posts in that area to get more traffic at much faster rates. I hope that makes sense.

No need to overthink this Google Analytics stuff, it's just something you want to check every now and then to know where your traffic is coming from.

Chapter 11: Payment Gateways

You're going to need to decide on a payment gateway, so if someone buys your info product, it automatically gets emailed to them. There are common Payment Gateways like Paypal or Stripe, and they can be found at Paypal.com or at Stripe.com. You should be able to set it up with your autoresponder so that when someone buys your info product, they simultaneously get put on your buyer's list for that product and automatically get sent an email with your product as an attachment, if it's a simple report or ebook. Just ask your autoresponder service's support how to set it up, and they'll walk you through what you need to do. That's what they're there for.

If it's a video course or something more complex it's going to have to exist on your website, so you'll need a WordPress plugin that can lock a page where your video course lies, which is a more complex setup and beyond the scope of this book. Though in order to point you in the right direction, to see what plugin I recommend for that, go here:

BloggerBlogger.com

Now, if you really wanted to get fancy, you can use the affiliate network payment gateway such as JVZoo, which can be found at JVZoo.com. In addition to serving as your payment gateway, your product can also be found on their market place, and also you can run your own affiliate program for it. Thus, if someone wanted to promote your product, you could set them up with an affiliate link, so they can get paid if they make a sale, and so that you can also get paid; it's a win-win situation for all. However, the affiliate network takes a small percentage of the sale for allowing you to make this happen.

There are plenty of affiliate network payment gateways out there, so feel free to search around for them and take your pick.

Chapter 12: The Strategy

So you should have your blog up, and have some affiliate banners on there. It's best to put those affiliate banners in your sidebar or footer, or both!

You should also have your product on there, as well as your lead magnet form, perhaps put both of these at the top of the sidebar above your affiliate banners. You will have to make your own banner for your product, which can be done on Canva for free, which can be found at:

Canva.com

However, for the lead magnet form, your autoresponder service should set you up with how to set that up. Again, contact their support, it's what you're paying them for after all.

So with your sidebar and footer monetized and your lead magnet form set up, all you need now is to get traffic to your blog, and that means writing blog posts as often as possible and getting on social media.

Though, this is only half the battle. Yes, there is another half we need to cover!

Chapter 13: The Strategy - Part 2

Okay, now for the second part of the strategy. Way back in Chapter 3 I told you it would be best to register with 3 to 6 affiliate programs at first and then register with more later, and finally we've come to the later part.

Basically, you should have your lead magnet people going onto one list, and you should have your info product buyers going on another list. And while your blog will make some money through people who purchase your info product and affiliate products, these lists that you are building is where the real money is made!

You should be emailing your list around 3 times a week, and in every single one of those emails, you want to let your list know about one of your new awesome blog posts! However, this list is not only for notifying your followers about blog posts, so only do that for your very best blog posts.

The reason anyone joins your list in the first place, is because they want info that they can't normally get from your blog. They want value, and they also expect you to keep them up-to-date on the latest ongoings in your niche, as well as let them know about any new products, because you're supposed to be the authority. They're all hoping you are actually the authority!

Anyway, so you need to provide your list with a ton of value they can't normally get on your blog. You need to share with your list the secret inside stuff that your followers can't get anywhere else! And every now and then you mention an affiliate offer. It's up to you how often you want to mention one, but don't be one of those bloggers who keeps hitting people up with the same offer again and again. You have got to offer up something new and exciting at least once every 2 weeks, or once a month at the very least.

The best way to learn how you should be emailing your list is to subscribe to your competitor's email lists.

Chapter 14: Trolls

No, I'm not referring to characters from fairy tales who live under bridges. As bloggers, the kinds of trolls we have to deal with are actually far worse!

A troll, as far as us bloggers are concerned, is a person who comes to your blog to write nasty comments and cause problems, because they enjoy upsetting others and the attention that goes along with it. And if you're lucky you may never get a troll. However, realistically speaking, you are sure to have your fair share of trolls.

When you get your first troll spouting off nasty comments, you'll be tempted to block them from commenting on your blog. And if what they say is obscene or would qualify as hate speech, then go ahead and block them.

However, if what they say is simply rude or offensive, but not anything completely obscene or would qualify as hate speech, then I would say engage with them. Be friendly, polite, and as courteous as you can possibly be and merely ignore the offensive characteristics of their comment, and just try to answer it as if it were a regular comment, and perhaps even end your comment with a question encouraging them to respond.

Basically, the more they comment on your blog posts, the more search engines will notice that your blog posts have activity going on, so the more likely your blog will rise in search engine results.

Thus, you want to embrace your trolls! Since as long as you have trolls who keep commenting, the more it will benefit your blog, especially early on when you're trying to grow your blog.

The fact of the matter is you'll have a lot more trolls later on, so it's good to start learning how to deal with them. Accept what they have to say as constructive criticism, but don't ever let it get you down or take it personally.

In fact, you should be thankful that you even have trolls, because the mere presence of trolls means your blog is growing. So don't worry about it, rather you should be happy, and you should love your trolls!

Chapter 15: Keep Posting

The fact of the matter is that all you really need to do to grow your blog is to keep writing blog posts. It's really the whole key to everything. Sure there are many ways to analyze it, and many things to consider, but aside from all of that, as long as you keep writing blog posts your blog will grow.

The reason that most blogs fail, is because the bloggers that run them fail to keep writing blog posts, so you don't want that to be you, just another failed useless blog taking up space on the Internet.

You have got to treat the process of writing and publishing blog posts like it is your mission in life, because the reality of things is that it is your mission in life!

I mean, how are you supposed to ever get to the point of becoming a million dollar blogger if you can't even maintain a sincere dedication to making regular blog posts! Seriously, this is what ends it for most people who could have probably grown there blogs into something great!

Because life throws many things at us, and it's very easy to take a break from writing blog posts to enjoy something or to try something else. Well, if you think like that, then it could very well be the end of your blog!

Your main thing you need to be trying to make is regular blog posts, the main thing you should be enjoying is writing and publishing regular blog posts. Because without a regular consistency of blog posts coming out of you, you've got nothing! You'd be just another washed up failed blogger with a dead blog.

Sure maybe you could make a little bit of income with a half-committed approach to blogging, but you won't be successful if your going for a million dollar blog if you maintain a half-committed approach kind of attitude.

You've got to face this fact, that you really need to be dedicated to blogging if you're ever going to grow. And how can you do that? How can you achieve the level of dedication I'm talking about? Well, the answer to that question is really simple: Keep Posting!

Chapter 16: Business Essentials

As soon as your blog makes a first sale, you're now officially a business.

Now my business advice in this chapter is very much my opinion, so don't base your business solely upon my advice. I just put it here for you to have a general idea of how you could set things up. Though, make sure you contact a professional business advisor, lawyer, or tax accountant before making any kinds of business decisions.

The rules of business will vary according to your country, province, or state. However, there are 2 general business structures that you can choose from that are pretty much similar across the board. And they are a sole proprietorship or a limited liability company, also known as an LLC. You'll need to check your local business laws about each.

Sole Proprietorship

Now if you're essentially strapped for cash, then the sole proprietorship will be the better move for you, and in many cases setting up a sole proprietorship is as simple as taking a stroll down to your local city office or city hall and filling out a form. They'll have to take a look at the form and stamp it and you're good to go! It's also possible to register for a sole proprietorship online without even visiting your city office, and again, this depends on where you live.

LLC

If you start as a sole proprietorship, that's fine. Though the moment you start earning an income equivalent to a full-time job, I would recommend upgrading to an LLC.

What the LLC does for you is it limits your liability if you were to get sued for some reason, because an LLC is considered to be a separate entity from you. Also, it just makes you look like you actually have a real business, because you can put the letters LLC after your business name.

In the U.S. an LLC can easily be registered for online. And I've put a link to the service I like to use to register an LLC at:

BloggerBlogger.com

Taxes

As a sole proprietorship or as an LLC, you're going to have to get used to doing your own taxes. And while doing your own taxes might seem like a chore, there are actually many benefits to it, such as the fact that you'll be able to deduct business expenses. Now, you don't have to do your own taxes, you could hire a tax accountant to do them for you, but it's really not so hard to use one of the many tax softwares available and just do them yourself. In case you're interested. I've got a link to the tax software I like to use at:

BloggerBlogger.com

Now, with the LLC, in the U.S. you could make a tax election for it to be treated as an S-Corp, which has certain tax benefits of being able to pay yourself dividends, or you could choose that it be treated as a passthrough entity. If you go the S-Corp route, you will most definitely need to hire a tax accountant, because it gets a lot more complicated. Though if you go the passthrough entity route, then you'll do just fine using tax software.

Trade Name

Now, another neat thing whether your a sole proprietorship or an LLC is that you'll be able to pick a trade name, also known as a DBA, which stands for Doing Business As. Now, the trade name could be your own name, or it could be the name of your blog, or any other kind of name you like. Using a trade name to conduct business under is simply one more thing that adds to the professionalism of your business. You'll want to check a trademark database to make sure that the trade name you want isn't already taken. I've got a link to the one I like to use at:

Trademark

Now, at some point, you eventually want to get a trademark for your trade name, and you also want to create a logo and get a trademark for your logo as well. A trademark is basically a protection for your business so that no one can steal your trade name. I've got a link to the place I like to use to get trademarks, at:

BloggerBlogger.com

Business Bank Account

You can run a sole proprietorship from a personal bank account, but if you are running an LLC you'll need a business bank account, because if you run an LLC from a personal bank it does something which is called piercing the veil of your LLC. Basically, since your LLC is a separate entity from you you need to keep all LLC income and expenses separate from your own. Anything you do to mix your LLC income or expenses with your own will pierce the veil. If you pierce the veil of your LLC, it renders your limited liability protection invalid, which kind of defeats one of the major reasons of starting an LLC in the first place.

To open a business bank account, I'd recommend calling

47

various banks and asking them about how to open a business checking account with them. With some, you can do the whole process over the phone and via email. With others, you'll actually have to go into the bank and bring some documents with you.

Chapter 17: The Right Look

If you check any million dollar blogger's blog, their blog posts are of a very high quality. Therefore, if you ever want to get to their level, then you need to create posts of a similar or better level of quality.

The quality of your posts is truly the key to making your blog stand out, so it deserves attention. I realize when you first start out, your posts may not be so great, but as you become accustomed to posting more and more, you also need to make an effort to improve your blog posts with each an every post. If you do that, then as you blog, your blog will not only grow by the number of posts you make, but will also grow in quality.

You essentially want to make each new post better than the last.

Not only that, you need to be doing the same with the look of your entire blog. Everytime you look at your blog, you want to be thinking about how you can improve it. You want to analyze your blog often and make little improvements week by week. And as time passes all of those little improvements will add up to something big.

Eventually, you'll end up with the right look, a very high quality and beautiful looking blog. That's exactly what we want! If our blog looks like a million bucks, then we're in a much better position to at some point make a million bucks!

Chapter 18: DMCA Takedown Notices

If you have an info product, you might be surprised one day to find out that someone copied it and is giving away downloads of it for free or selling it at a discounted price.

However, before you get this little surprise, you want to prepare for this eventuality, and you want to shut down anyone who is giving away your product the moment they start giving it away.

So the first thing you need to do is set up a Google alert. Just go to:

Google.com/Alerts

And set up and create an alert for your product's name. That way Google can alert you when your product appears somewhere where it's not supposed to.

Now, when it does happen, and your product does appear for download somewhere that is not your site. Then it's time to issue a DMCA takedown notice. DMCA stands for Digital Millennium Takedown Act, and it's basically a sort of legal notice that you would send to a website to have them take down the download links to the unauthorized copy of your product.

Also, you'll want to request that the page for the product be removed from both Google and Bing, so that people can't find it in their search results.

For information on how to construct and send a DMCA takedown notice and how to request that Google and Bing remove the page from their search engine, just go to:

BloggerBlogger.com

Now of course once you're making big money as a blogger you could have a lawyer take care of these issues for you, but until then it's not that difficult to take care of them yourself.

Chapter 19: The Road Ahead

Now, you basically know everything you need to know to move forward on your journey to becoming a million dollar blogger.

The road ahead is one riddled with challenges galore. And you must face them with courage, honor, and valor.

There will be many a time when you'll face a challenge so great it will make you think about giving up. It's imperative that you do not give up when this challenge presents itself to you. You must look the challenge in the eye and shout at the top of your lungs, "I am on a path to becoming a million dollar blogger and I will defeat you!" And then tackle the challenge.

If you don't succeed at first don't give up, keep on tackling the challenge until you triumph. Of course if it's a very mighty challenge, it's okay to take a break to have some tea. Though don't just sit on your rear end drinking tea all day, because you have no choice but to slay the challenge!

I would recommend you don't just stop at this blogging book, but continue to read more blogging books. Because the fact of the matter is that there is always something to learn, even if you think you are reading about something you already know, sometimes you may just find a golden nugget of info in there that changes the way you do things.

As the blogosphere is always changing, there are always new pieces of knowledge that can aid you on your quest. Therefore, it's good to always be learning. Never stop learning.

And I should also mention that I'd recommend you join my secret blogging newsletter. You can find it at:

BloggerBlogger.com

I've got a free bonus for those who join that I think should greatly help you on your journey. Not only that, but you'll also receive critical updates about the blogosphere from me as well as news about new blogging tools and strategies. Therefore, if you want to stay in the know, it's to your benefit to join.

Chapter 20: Advanced Strategies

Now, we'll get into some advanced strategies you should most definitely implement.

Keep Creating Info Products

It's great to have an info product, but you're going to want to create more info products. You eventually want a whole selection of info products for your followers to choose from. Never stop creating info products, keep working on creating more. Once a month would be great, or at least once every 3 months.

Offer A Launch Week Discount

Everytime you launch a new info product, you want to do a discount for the week you launch it, and email your entire list to let them know that you just launched a new product and it will be offered at a discount during launch week.

Put Affiliate Links In Your Info Products And Lead Magnet

I'd also recommend putting affiliate links inside your info products, as well as inside your lead magnet for products related to the info product or lead magnet. This will allow you to monetize things one step further.

Join An Affiliate Network

An affiliate network is a site where numerous product creators and affiliates work together to sell their products. Which affiliate network you join would be largely dependent on your niche.

For any business related niches JVZoo and WarriorPlus are good ones. For all other niches, Clickbank is a good one. However, there are many other affiliate networks you can find by searching for the keywords "affiliate network" in a search engine.

The good part about joining an affiliate network is that you can use its large database of affiliate products to promote to your list. You only need to register with an affiliate network once and that basically gives you access to all of its products, but you may need to request permission from the product creator to promote their product.

Another good thing about an affiliate network is that you can put your products on them, and other affiliate marketers can then promote your products. Not to mention the fact that you can use the affiliate network's buy button as your payment gateway.

Get Good With Your Autoresponder

Since emailing your list is where most of your income will come from, you want to really take the time to go through all of the tutorials of your autoresponder and master it.

Really Try To Make One Blog Post A Day

The reality of the matter is your going to see the fastest growth if you can make one blog post a day, and since time is precious, you may as well try to grow as fast as you can, so see if you can aim for a blog post a day!

Start A Youtube Channel

The reality is that it's easier to rank for keywords on Youtube than it is on Google, and Youtube videos will also rank quite well on Google. Plus Youtube just makes for an awesome source of traffic. You could just do one Youtube video a week on a topic related to one of your blog posts, and make sure to leave a link in the description of your video to your blog post, though if you can Youtube 3 times a week it's much better.

Chapter 21: Support Request

As you are now a fellow blogger like myself, I would like to issue a support request to you. And that request is that if this book helped you out in any capacity, then I would request that you go ahead and leave a review for this book.

Reviews help contribute to the ecosystem, to keep the good books on top and the bad books on bottom. And they also help let us authors know what we did right, so that we can provide you with better content.

And anyway, if you've read this far, then you know what you think of this book better than anyone, so I'd love to read your review.

Thank you, and until next time.

www.ingramcontent.com/pod-product-compliance
Lightning Source LLC
Chambersburg PA
CBHW072016230526
45468CB00021B/1625